# Conversations with God: Book 3

Matthew Robert Payne

Please visit http://personal-prophecy-today.com to sow into Matthew's writing ministry, to request a personal prophecy or life coaching, or to contact him.

Cover designed by akira007 at fiverr.com.

Edited by Lisa Thompson at www.writebylisa.com You can email Lisa at writebylisa@gmail.com for your editing needs.

The opinions expressed by the author are not necessarily those of Revival Waves of Glory Books & Publishing.

Published by Revival Waves of Glory Books & Publishing PO Box 596 Litchfield, Illinois 62056 USA

Revival Waves of Glory Books & Publishing is committed to excellence in the publishing industry. Their website is www.revivalwavesofgloryministries.com Book design Copyright © 2017 by Revival Waves of Glory Books & Publishing. All rights reserved.

Paperback: 978-1-68411-475-7

Hardcover: 978-1-387-40583-1

# Dedication

I want to dedicate this book to my close friend, Andrea, from New Zealand. I look forward to speaking to her each week over the phone. Andrea, you have read many of my books and through reading them, you have come to know me well. I am so pleased that you are my friend, and you love me for who I am. I know that you have read my memoir, *His Redeeming Love: A Memoir*. I enjoy speaking with you and knowing you. You have been good to me, laughing with me, drawing me out of myself, and helping me to fly. You are such a kind friend to me.

I hope that as you read this dedication, you see in print that I love you and respect you for who you are and for who you have been to me.

# Acknowledgements

I want to thank my mother and father for all the love that they have given me. I want to thank Jesus, the Father, and the Holy Spirit for being part of my life and for leading me. I want to thank all of my friends who love and support me. I want to thank Bill Vincent from Revival Waves of Glory Books & Publishing for publishing my book and the people who have sown into my ministry to make it possible for me to publish this book.

This book is the third in my series, Conversations with God. I followed many of the subjects in *Jesus Speaking Today*.

I want to thank you, the reader, for deciding to buy this book and for believing in me enough to read it. I hope that you have been blessed by some of my books already. If this is the first book of mine that you have read, I hope that this book will encourage you to read more of my books.

# Table of Contents

Dedication ............................................................3

Acknowledgements ................................................4

Introduction.........................................................6

A Note from My Editor .........................................7

Message 1 - Consistency .......................................8

Message 2 - Worship.............................................13

Message 3 - Revelation .........................................19

Message 4 - Glorify Me .........................................24

Message 5 - Be Connected ....................................29

Message 6 - Be Thankful .......................................33

Message 7 - Carrying Burdens................................38

Message 8 - Feeling Down.....................................43

Message 9 - Trust and Obey ..................................48

Message 10 - The Journey .....................................54

Message 12 - Trouble ...........................................65

Message 13 - Patience...........................................71

Message 14 - Life Dreams .....................................76

I'd love to hear from you.......................................81

How to Sponsor a Book Project...............................82

Other Books by Matthew Robert Payne .....................83

About Matthew Robert Payne .................................85

# Introduction

I welcome you to this book. This is the third book in my series of *Conversations with God*. I started out a little nervous in the first book in the series. But with these conversations in this book, I am a lot more comfortable recording my dialogues with God.

Through posting all of these conversations with God on my blog and through sharing them on Facebook, I have become aware that people really enjoy reading what God has to say to me. Keeping in mind that people are really blessed by my personal conversations with God, I spent the money to produce this book.

In the past month, I produced a book, *How to Hear God's Voice: Keys to Two-Way Conversational Prayer*, in which I teach people how to hear from God. As you read this book and these personal conversations that I had with God, it is my prayer that you too would pursue God and start to journal your own conversations with him.

I commend this book to you.


Matthew Robert Payne

November 2017

# A Note from My Editor

God speaks to Matthew in this little book as a friend to a friend. The Father's heart is so evident for Matthew, and his words are so filled with love. While some might think that they could never attain this type of relationship with the Father, Jesus, and the Holy Spirit, the Bible is clear that the triune God desires such intimacy with each of us.

Even under the old covenant, God spoke with both Abraham and Moses as friends. (See James 2:23 and Exodus 33:11.) How much more will he do for us who are under a new covenant, blood-bought believers and brothers of Jesus! Jesus tells us in John 15:15 that he no longer called the disciples servants but called them friends.

Matthew demonstrates that deep level of friendship and connection with God that these men of old had with him. Truly, God's heart is to speak with each of us in this way.

May this book encourage you to pursue this intimacy for yourself by beginning two-way conversations with each member of the Trinity.

If you have any writing, editing, or proofreading questions, I am happy to help. See my website at www.writebylisa.com or email me at writebylisa@gmail.com for more information.


God bless you, dear reader.

Lisa

# Message 1 - Consistency

God:

How are you today?

Matthew:

I didn't have much sleep last night, so I went to bed today and slept all day. Now it is eleven o'clock p.m., and I am wide awake. You started talking to me in bed, and I decided to get up and do a new post from you.

God:

It is so exciting to speak to you. I am glad for all the ways that I can speak to you. You saw an advertisement for whisky as you walked to the shop, and I told you that you are better to us than the best whisky up here. You were touched. I am so glad that you are so open to hearing us through whatever means we choose to speak to you.

Matthew:

I am an open book to you guys. I am always open to what you have to say. Even so, at times, I have decided that I will sin, and I don't want to hear anything to the contrary. But that doesn't happen too often these days.

God:

I am glad that you spoke about that exception when you are not open to us speaking. That shows that you are, first, human, and second, you are honest with me and others. I like that about you, Matthew. When you are led by the Holy Spirit, you are always honest. You are consistently honest. Consistency is a good character trait. For instance, you don't carry cash very often, but we know that when you do, we can encourage you to give money to the poor on the streets that are begging. I know that you will always ask us how much to give to the person. You are not only prepared to give, but you are prepared to give whatever we say.

Matthew:

Well, you know the needs of the poor. You know how much they need, and you know how much others will give to them. I remember the time that you told me to take a beggar to lunch and to give him $20. We enjoyed a wonderful lunch, and we had a great conversation. He told me that you always look after him. I was blessed and impacted more than that man that day.

God:

I love to have people that I can depend on to feed my people. I love to have people with soft hearts that are full of compassion. I love to move on people's hearts via my Holy Spirit to give. I love to move on my people's hearts to show love to each other. I love to have people that are loving and compassionate. I wish that all people flowed with my compassion.

The lady at Toastmasters attacked you this week for your belief in Jesus. She was rude and very forceful with you, having you give reasons as to why you love Jesus.

I told you to witness to her and to be your loving self, but she probably won't ever give her life to Jesus. When I told you that, you were upset for her. You have a hard time accepting that your influence in another person's life won't bear fruit for the kingdom.

Here, I have repeated myself for you. You know now how she stands. You know now that she will likely always be estranged from me. You can still be gracious to her, but you don't have to compromise yourself or bow to her in any way because your actions will never result in her coming to repentance.

I have not told you the destiny of the others in your group as I want you to be Jesus to all of them. I use you to sow seeds of love to people. I use you all the time to show people my love and grace.

But when it comes to this woman, I don't need you to do her any favors. She has a controlling spirit and is ruled by evil, so I don't want you to be weak around her. I want you to be a man. I want you to be able to speak up if she needs it, and I want to use that as a witness to the others.

The people in your Toastmaster's group need to know that a Christian does not need to be walked over. I was very upset the other night when she lashed out at you. You were even considering not going back to Toastmasters in the midst of it. That is what the devil wanted.

I need you to be love and grace to the people. I need you to be light and salt. I need you to speak for me and Christians. I have a great heart for the others in the group. I want you to be my love to them. I want you to consistently show my love to them.

You will notice that one of the men wasn't very loving when she was lashing out at you, but when she left, he was loving again. Don't hold that against him. Her controlling spirit is affecting him. Don't worry about how he acts when she is around. He can't be himself. But when she is gone, you will have this man's attention.

I admire you for speaking out about Donald Trump and how, of all the choices, you want him to be president. Most of them have harsh things to say against him, but I admire your courage to speak up in defense of the man I want to be president.

This is what I want you to be among these Toastmasters. I want you to be an authentic, loving, well-balanced Christian. I want you to stand up for righteousness. I want you to be my light. You might never see them make a decision for me while you are among them, but I am using you to shed my light and grace upon them.


Matthew:

I am so happy that you are going to use me to influence them. I don't need to know that they made a decision for you. I just want to be light to them. I just want to be your joy and your peace.

I am heartbroken about this woman, but I can see that you want me to be confident around her and not be weak. I can see that you want me to be vocal if she reacts negatively again. I will take note of that. I see that my strong stance will also be a witness to the others that will be listening. I have to say that I prefer to know her eventual outcome so that I have a strategy in advance.

I have to say that I enjoy you speaking to me. I am sure that everyone that reads this book can see from this post that you have worthwhile things to say to people if they would only learn to listen.


God:

I love you, Matthew, as you are so wise. I love the way that you move in our wisdom. I love that I can speak to you, and you clearly discern what I am saying, even reading between the lines. I love that you can hear me speaking to you, and you can see a vision in your mind of a confrontation with her where you stand your ground. I want you to move with my wisdom and always come to me for fresh understanding.

I have all the answers for people if they would only seek me and ask me what I want to say to them and the way that I want them to go. I know the best routes for people. I have the best answers. I have the best direction and decisions for them. It is my hope that this series of books will lead people to seek me out and allow me to personally speak to them.

I want to lead my church. I want to lead people individually. Yes, I want leaders and will never replace them, but I want my army to be able to follow my leading all by themselves. I want to lead my people out. I want my army to take ground from the enemy. I want my army to go behind enemy lines to places like Toastmasters where there is no other Christian voice, and I want them to bring my righteousness and my light to those places. I want the Christians of the world to touch those that are suffering and dying in this harsh world that you live in.

I personally want my church to be consistent in their love and in their compassion. And I want my people to be strong with morals and grace in equal measure. According to Amos 5:24, I want to raise up a standard in the land so that when the enemy comes in, like a flood, my righteousness will flow over them.

Be blessed, Matthew. Thanks for sitting down to listen to me.


Matthew:

Thanks, God.

# Message 2 - Worship

God:

How are you today?

Matthew:

I have had a productive day so far. I am feeling pretty good. I just had a person write a nice comment on my latest post from you. I was so encouraged by it that I am here again to speak to you.

God:

Once again, you have put on some worship music, and you are listening to my voice. I love you so much. Just like you love this song that is playing, I love you heaps more. I love you so much. You are very special to me.

Matthew:

You are always telling me how you love me. Honestly, your love never fails in my life. I love how you speak to me. Today, we are speaking about worship.

I am a little different than most people. I usually sit down through the worship songs at church because I have a sore leg. Sometimes I stand up.

But worship isn't as much about an hour at church once a week to me. Instead, worship is found in walking in your ways. My life and my actions are my worship of you.

I think if people realized that they can call everything that they do in life for you worship, then their opinion of how much they worship you would change.


God:

People have different ideas of what worship is and what it constitutes. Yes, you live a lifestyle of worship and obedience to me. To me, that is real worship.

Some people assume that they have to be singing to worship me. They can worship me simply by thanking me; they can worship by simply thinking of me. People can worship me by being my love to the world.

You are one of the fortunate ones that walk with a measure of my presence each day. Not many people live with a strong presence and an awareness of me throughout their day. You live your life being led by my Holy Spirit and by doing almost everything we want you to do each day.

In Matthew 15:8, Jesus said, "These people . . . honor Me with their lips, but their hearts are far from Me."

It is sad but true that many people don't live with an awareness of me each day. Some people only think of me on Sunday, and for the rest of the week, I am left out in the cold. I want to be present in people's minds. I want the hearts of people.

Your heart is for me. You have a pure heart. You have a heart that wants to do everything that I want. Your whole life is centered on me and what I want to do through you. You prepared two books in the last few weeks and when led by us, you put them aside to focus on the books that we wanted.

Many people cannot be led like that. Many people make decisions and ask us to bless them. But you are led by us. I love that about you.

Your heart is steadfastly on us and on our will every single day. Sure, you do things that might not be in our perfect will. You are not a robot taking directions from us all day, but you are free to do what you like with your time, your money, and your energy. It just seems that most of what you do is what we wanted you to do. You are led in total freedom by our Spirit. You are free to do what you want, yet most of the time, you do what we want.

That is how I wish that people would operate. That is how I wish the church would operate. That would make the once-a-week praise and worship more fulfilling and beautiful as people come to church each week, gather with the brethren, and celebrate the work that has been accomplished for my glory during the week.

Not many people understand this concept of worship. They have not been taught this. They have not been taught that working to do my will each day is the highest form of worship that they can bring me.

Of course, it is especially sweet to me to be worshipped when a person is going through suffering and hard times. Hearing the sacrifice of praise from a hurting person is such sweet music to my ears.

For much of your life, you have been suffering with mental illness and a sin-ridden way of life. It is really exciting to draw you to myself, to touch and heal you. It is remarkable to use you as a writer now to lift people's hearts and encourage them. You have such an amazing story to share. The depths of your wisdom are astounding to some people. And the exciting thing about all of it is that you are truly thankful and happy for your life and who you have been made to be.

I look at you and see your life, and I bring others around me, and we sing songs about you. I sing over you. I love you so much, my sweetheart.

I thank myself for you. I thank you for being you. You have fallen in sin lately, yet I am restoring your strength. We will not let the devil have the victory for as long as he would like it.


Matthew:

I am so happy that you are pleased with me. I know that I have had a hard life, but I thank you for sending your Son into my life to be my friend. Jesus has been so good to me. I praise you for everything that you are doing in my life. I am so touched that you would speak to me.


God:

Are you kidding me?

There is nothing I would rather do than speak to you. You are a delight to me. I love you so much. I know that the English language is too limited to convey the feelings that I have for you.

I trip over myself to speak to you. I long to speak to you. I love to be with you. I love for you to type my words. You are so special to me. I long to have you in heaven more and more. In the future, I will have you continue to visit the council in heaven. A grievous wound was given to you by the enemy, but you will come once again to meet with the council.

Here is heaven and your coffee shop in your house. Seated in the chairs around the table are the saints of the galactic council. They are all waving to you. You are loved so much. They all love you. They are all going to start to visit you on earth from now on to rebuild your confidence. And in the right time, you can come once again to the meeting place and continue your blog.

On another subject, do you know that worship songs in heaven were written about you? Do you know that we sing songs up here about you?

Matthew:

No, I didn't know that.

God:

Through watching your life and interacting with you, Michael Jackson has written a song about what it is like to be a model Christian with a pure and humble heart. It is a wonderful song.

Do you know when heaven heard that song, the people of heaven stopped what they were doing and wept?

Just like you are weeping now. It is a masterpiece.

Michael is an extraordinary musician. He captured your essence in a way that made the people of heaven recently vote that song as the number one song in heaven.[1]

Do you know how very special you are to us?

Matthew:

I am overcome with emotion.

---

[1] Heaven holds two contests each week to see who can write the best contemporary song and the best worship song. All the people of heaven then vote on which song will win as the top song in each category. This is what God is referring to when he told Matthew that Michael wrote a number one song about him. You can find more information about this in Matthew's book, *Michael Jackson Speaks from Heaven*.

God:

You stand out here. When you come to heaven, people are shocked to see you. Every single saint in heaven wants to meet you. That is why we have a chain of coffee shops in heaven named after you. In the future, much of your time in heaven will be spent talking to the people of heaven and hugging them. And when you give a lecture, stadiums of people will listen to you.

That is why we have an arena in the galactic council room. They are waiting for you to teach.

Yes, you are a little person on earth with two thousand people that buy your books each month, but you are by no means little in heaven. Michael has only written two songs that became number one in heaven. One was about Jesus, and the second one was about you.

I want you to remember this when you are having a hard time on earth and the devil is attacking you and pulling you down. I want you to remember this conversation. I want you to remember that you have a hit song that has been written about you.

Saints collect paintings of you by your sister and other artists in heaven. Saints are lining up for the paintings from your sister after speaking to you. You really have to visit the council again when you are ready and emotionally up to it.

I will bid you good night. Be at peace, Matthew.

# Message 3 - Revelation

God:

How are you today?

Matthew:

I slept a lot yesterday. I was awakened in the middle of the night tonight. I felt led to not just check my email but to stay up. About half an hour ago, you told me that you were going to do another conversation with me. So here we are.

God:

It is so good to speak to you. I love speaking with you. I love that you are led by my Spirit. I love how you flow with the direction from the Holy Spirit. I also love having one-on-one time with you and speaking directly to you like this.

Matthew:

It has been fun getting to know you. I never knew you well. All of my life, I have dealt with Jesus, and I see now that you both are very much alike. I enjoy it when you speak to me. I am overjoyed that the Creator of the universe wants to speak to me. It is such fun to write down your words and record what you have to say. I am humbled. You humble me.

God:

You do a great job of humbling yourself. You have the choice to grow proud of your achievements with thirty published books now, but still, you remain humble and low to the ground. Through your humility, you remain open to us and what we want to tell you.

Matthew:

I have seen how ugly and distasteful pride is. I never want to let myself become that. I am happy that you see me as humble. You have used your prophetic voices to speak that message to me time and time again. You are happy with my humility. I guess we learn from a position of humility.

God:

Yes, in humility you remain teachable and open to new revelation. When you were interviewing a saint from heaven, he said: "The meaning of life is finding out your purpose and doing it with such excellence that you bring glory to God."

Matthew:

Yes, that has rocked my world. I wish that the whole word could read that and learn it well. It was so important to me. A lot of my message is encouraging people to find out their life purpose and walk in it while they are alive. I was so impressed with that quote, and I have repeated it a number of times since in my books.

God:

That is what revelation will do to you. It will change you and move you in a different direction. It will impact you in a great way. You like to do things with excellence. You love to live out your purpose. That meant so much to you. When the doubts came in about that encounter with a saint from heaven, if it really happened, you know that you have that quote to reassure you that you did not make up those words — the words that are full of wisdom.

Matthew:

Yes that is true. I will never forget that conversation. I really love receiving revelation.

God:

The same was true when we showed you that those that do the will of God are those that are not going to be denied by Jesus on the final day. We showed you that denying the world and its lusts and following the leading of the Holy Spirit will assure you that you go to heaven.

Many people fear the words of Jesus in Matthew 7:23, "Depart from me, I never knew you," and they live part of their Christian life in fear that Jesus might say those words to them. Once we showed you that doing my will and coming out of the world and its lusts will assure you of your place in heaven, it brought great peace to you.

Matthew:

Yes, that was an example of revelation that cleared up things for me. I love it when your Holy Spirit breathes on your Word and makes it come alive. I love it when your Holy Spirit makes your Word mean more and jump off the page into my spirit.

James 4:4 says that friendship with the world makes you an enemy of God. This is a key verse about making it to heaven. I saw how you really illuminated that verse to me. You had me ask the question, "How many people can remain an enemy of God and make it to heaven?"

When you bring revelation, it is not like reading a book. It hangs around and impacts the rest of your life. You can forget knowledge over time, but I don't think that you can forget revelation.

God:

That is why it is so important for people to read the Word and let us speak to them. A person can share a revelation in a book, but unless that revelation hits home to you, it remains just knowledge to be read and forgotten. People should come to us and allow us to bring revelation to them.

I realize that you were hurt by people teaching you error, Matthew, and you don't like to read the verses that people used to teach you error. We know that you have been hurt by these people, and it has affected your Bible reading, but we understand you and will work with you.

The recent revelation about Matthew 7:23 and the answer to what Jesus meant when he said, "Depart from me, I never knew you," rocked you, and you have shared that since. It is your prayer that people catch this revelation.

I would love to reveal more of myself and my wisdom to people if they would only take the time to come and spend time with me.

Here is one for you:

I love people far more than they even love themselves, and a person does not realize how much I love them until they get to heaven and live there. I even love proud people and will act in their lives to humble them and let them know who they really are to me.

Matthew:

That is sweet. I thought that was the case. I don't really understand how much you love me. I think you said once in a prophecy that if I knew how much you loved me that I would never worry again. It would be a wonderful life if I had no worry. I knew when the person prophesied that to me that I needed to come to understand more fully how much you love me.

I am so happy that you pursue me. I have let you and Jesus down so many times, and it astounds me that all my sin has been forgiven. You guys have so much patience, which is quite amazing to me. You not only love me, but you trust me with your wisdom and revelation.


God:

We simply see your potential. We simply love you in a pure way. We don't look at your actions and how you fall short; we look at your heart condition. You have a pure heart, Matthew, one that makes us sing for joy. That is why you are a writer so that you can help others become like you.

Now, you enjoy the rest of your night. Goodbye.


Matthew:

Goodbye, Lord.

# Message 4 - Glorify Me

God:

How are you doing today?

Matthew:

I have a backwards sleeping pattern. I am awake half the night and sleep in during the day. I am trying not to let it get to me.

God:

It is so good to see you and speak to you. It has been quite a while since you sat down and spoke to me. It has been a really long time, yet you have spoken to my Son quite a bit in this season.

I put a longing in your heart today to speak to me. I like to direct your paths. I like to lead you in what to do. You are in a tender place. You have a book about hearing me speak that is proving hard to do, which has you concerned. You are constantly having to rest in me and draw on my strength through the Holy Spirit. Your life is a continual walk of patience.

Things don't always come easy to you. Just like now, you are waiting on other people to complete the books that you are working on. This frustration that you have has to be brought to us.

Can you imagine just how we feel about the world? Can you imagine that we have to rely on other people for our will to be done on earth? You are waiting on your friend Craig, your editor, Lisa, and your typist to type, yet we are waiting on millions and millions of people to do what we want them to do.

You run to us for comfort to deal with the frustration. Who do we run to with our frustration? Have you ever thought about that? I have Jesus to convey my feelings to, and we have a few saints up here that can help shoulder some of our burdens, but even for us, life can be hard.

I don't think people consider that about us. I don't think people really understand our feelings and what we go through. You need patience, and you are just dealing with three people, and we have millions, even billions, that we are waiting on.

I needed to speak to you today. I needed to share my heart with you. I need a friend. I need you to think about the bigger picture. The three books that the three people are working on will touch many lives. Yet I want to touch the whole world and bring them to my Son's cross.


Matthew:

I am happy that I came to see you today. Don't cry, Father. Your tears touch me.


God:

I need the people of the world to know that I hurt also. I need people to consider what I go through. I need people to get to know me and come and be my friend. I need more friends.


Matthew:

Craig wants to teach people how to be your friend. I hope he does a great job. I hope that he brings a lot of people to you. I only have a small reach now. A lot of people are not reading these books of mine. I wish that I could speak to the world for you. I wish that I could teach others how to feel like I do. I wish that I could teach people how to glorify you with their lives.

The world can be such a hard place in which to live. So many things are happening. People have so many concerns. Not many people think of you all the time or live their lives to do your will.

God:

You are just a little person. You are just a person with one talent, but you have really put that talent to work. Your life is a miracle that testifies of me. People really love you and are touched by how far you have come.

You have overcome so much. You struggled all your life with certain sins, and now, they are in the past. You failed English in school, yet here you are, a writer who is publishing a new book nearly every six weeks. You are doing everything that we wanted you to do.

Your life is an advertisement for us and our grace and power. Anyone that reads your books comes to know Jesus and how powerfully he has worked in your life. You are a showpiece, and when you become more popular, your testimony will set many people free.

Elements of your life are still deficient. You have a messy house; you lack good clothes, and you do not have a good diet. People who get close to you can see these things. As Diana said to you, this is because you have stopped caring about some things. We will bring healing into your life so that those things can be corrected.

But to the people that read your books and read what you post on Facebook, you are a great guy that shines with the light of Jesus. Your life glorifies us.

You worry sometimes about what you are going to write in all the books that we have planned for your life. But when you catch yourself worrying, you quickly think that this need has been addressed by the Holy Spirit, and he has not let you down so far.

Many times, you divert back to the Holy Spirit to carry you through. This is what it really means to walk in the Holy Spirit. You need to let him empower and carry you. In this way, you do the impossible, and the people watching your life really witness a miracle. We want the people to see the impossible done through you so that they would also learn to lean on the Holy Spirit for themselves instead of trusting and relying on their flesh.


Matthew:

It is true. I often have to rely on the Holy Spirit. I have some patience, but sometimes it is stretched. I have some love, but when people come against me, it is stretched. In every area of my life, I am being stretched. I have to continually rely on the Holy Spirit. I am so happy that he helps me.


God:

With you, Matthew, I can sit face to face and speak plainly, but my church most often does not know my voice, let alone have the time to listen to me. My sadness is overwhelming and almost all-consuming.

With most of my church, I cannot sit down face to face with them. Most of my church can't hear me. That is why your book with Craig is so important, and the devil is giving you so much grief about it. Satan does not want that book published. He is trying everything that he can to make you give up on it.

Please come to me more often. I need you, my friend.

Thanks for obeying the leading of the Holy Spirit and coming tonight to speak with me.

Matthew:

What else could I do? I am directed by you guys. I love you, Father.

(Gives God a hug)

Bye.


God:

Bye, my friend.

# Message 5 - Be Connected

God:

How are you doing?

Matthew:

I can't sleep, so I thought I would get up and speak to you and record what you have to say. I have not been going to church too often, so this is a weird subject for me at this moment.

God:

Every day, you connect with your friends on Facebook. Every day, you chat on Skype and through Facebook, message people. Whenever you feel guilty, that feeling does not come from my Holy Spirit. You have lots of fellowship with people overseas. You are not a lone ranger. You do not act or make decisions without consulting your friends and consulting my Spirit.

You have a very deep relationship with my Son and the Holy Spirit. Every day, they are with you, advising and leading you. Nearly everything that you do is inspired by the Holy Spirit. My Spirit has so much sway in your life. You are a model Christian, and I am so proud of you.

Matthew:

It warms my heart to hear that you think I am a model Christian. I try to be. I try to be led by the Holy Spirit in all that I do. It is so much fun to be led by you and your Spirit. I know that you have commissioned every book that I produce. I enjoy doing what you put on my heart to do.

It makes me happy that I make you proud. I know that when I prophesy and tell people that Jesus is proud of them, they are touched. They write to me and comment that those words touched them. It is truly a great thing to know that you are proud of me.

I am just a simple person. Many people look up to me and think that I am someone amazing and that I have this great relationship with you. I simply have tried my best to draw close to Jesus throughout my life. In a way, I didn't really have a choice. For most of my life, I have had few if any friends, and I have really needed to be close to Jesus.

Through all the ups and downs and all the stress, Jesus has been my rock. He has been my security and my friend. Through him, I have come to meet you. One day, as clear as light comes in a sunrise, he took me to meet you. I will never forget it. You treated me like your favorite son and welcomed me with open arms.


God:

I loved that day when you came to meet me. I had been looking forward to that and watching you all of your life. I watched you accept my Son. I saw you struggle with addictions. I saw you grow close to my Son and begin to become very obedient to his directions and requests. I watched you grow to trust him with all of your life.

One day, when the time was right, Jesus introduced me to you. You had grown up with an angry father, so you had a distorted view of who I was. On that day, we spoke. Right away, you prayed for your older brother, and I showed you that I would take care of him. Right now, your brother is suffering, yet I know you hold onto my reaction to your first prayer for him. I will do great things for your brother at the right time when he has been humbled like I want to humble him.

In John 14:6, Jesus said that the only way to me was through him. You found out on that day that it was true. Surely, Jesus was the door to my heart and to meeting me.

It is so good to speak to you, my son. I enjoy you. I watch everything that you do on earth. I see each conversation. I see every interaction that you have with people. I feel every time that you are hurt. I see and feel your every frustration. I feel your heart and your emotions.

Not only do you feel my heart and my emotions, but I feel yours. You are important to me. I am going to use you in the future to speak for me and Jesus. I am going to use you as my spokesman. I will put my words in your mouth, and you will boldly speak them.

I am going to bring more friends into your life. I am going to bring you company one day. I am going to lead you. You will not always be alone. I have to be careful with who I bring into your life as we want you to come to us first when it comes to your life and your decisions. You and I know that if you had many friends over the past twenty years that you would not be as close to us as you are now.

We have kept you hidden and set apart for us and for our purposes. We don't want lukewarm friends in your life, and it is quite hard to find you friends that are as passionate as you are. Do you understand that?


Matthew:

Yes, I understand that. I understand that you have had me set apart, and I know that I would not be as close to you if I had lots of friends. The fact that I am alone makes me press into you. The fact that I don't have people in my life helps me to stay really connected to you guys.

I can see the benefit of traveling the life that I have traveled. I can see your wisdom through all of it. I praise you and lift up your name as I know that it is your wisdom that has made me into the person that I am today.

My relationship with Jesus isn't new. It is not just a few months old. It has been strong for years and years, and I have all that testimony to fall back on and share. You guys treat me so well.

Thanks for the conversation today.


God:

It was fun. It is always great to talk to you. Take care. I hope you can go to bed soon. You are a joy to me. Remember that I am proud of you.

# Message 6 - Be Thankful

God:

This is a rigged question. I know the answer, but the readers don't know it. How are you today?

Matthew:

I am not in a good place. I have had indigestion for about twelve hours today. I seem to be getting it almost every day, and the tablets don't seem to be working for me like they used to. It is hard to cope with, and I am little worried about my health. I am so worried that I am going to the doctor about it.

God:

You looked up the subject in your book, *Jesus Speaking Today*, to see what subject we were on and what we had to cover. I saw you try to decide against doing this post.

But you don't need to think about praising me when everything is going well. Likewise, you should not dwell on what is bad when life is hard for you.

I think that our talk today is going to cheer you up a little, which is why the Holy Spirit gave you the idea of sitting down with me and starting this conversation. You need to stop and think about the blessings in your life and be thankful.

Matthew:

If I do that, will you take the pain away?

God:

Ha, ha. You are funny.


Matthew:

I just got off the phone with my publisher and he is going to arrange to translate my books into Spanish for $100 U.S. That is an amazing price. I am so thankful that you led me to him. He has published more than twenty-five of my books, and he does a great job. I honestly don't think that I could have done everything that I have done if it were not for him.

I would not have hardcover or audio books if it were not for him. So many people buy my books in those formats, and it is all because of him. I love Bill, and with fifty books of his own, he knows all about the effort that goes into books.

Thank you for leading me to him years ago. I love you for that. Thank you so much for Bill. He is even going to reduce the prices of all my books to ninety-nine cents. I could not change the prices of some of those books on my own. I am so touched that you put it on his heart to ask me if I wanted to change the prices of all my books to ninety-nine cents.

You are a wonderful God. You not only show me favor so that I can earn money by giving prophecies, sharing angel messages, and having people donate to me, but you change the heart of my publisher to offer to make my books inexpensive for the readers to buy.


God:

Everything that is important to you is important to me. You are my friend, and I care about you and your desires. Thank you for thanking me. I enjoy having a thankful friend.

In heaven, we hear a lot of angry people who are upset with us. When people are blessed, they think they did it themselves, and when things go bad, we are blamed for it.

You might think that sitting down with me is good for you. You might think that sitting down with me helps your readers. But I want to tell you that when you sit down with me, it really blesses my heart.

I am really blessed to be able to speak my heart to you and to your readers. I have so many things to say and to get off my chest. I wish that I could speak heart to heart with people that know and serve me. I could accomplish so much more on earth if people could actually hear me. People would change how they view me if they could hear me speak.

I love coming to sit in your house. Your presence moves me to tears. I am just so thankful to be your friend. You might not think that I need friends, but I really do. It is so refreshing to meet someone with no agenda. It is so rewarding to see your angel or the Holy Spirit speak to you and see you do what they ask without question. It is so good to have a friend that listens to us.

You have been thinking that with thirty books that it is time for you to come home. You have reached a stage where you have finally come into rest. You have reached a stage where you are not striving and where you think you have said and written enough. You are happy with the job that you have done in life. You don't need to prove anything to anyone anymore. You are content and at peace. Even your pain seems to have left as you type this.

I am thankful for you. I love you so much. I sit opposite you on a couch, and my eyes are full of tears. Your presence and your love bring me to tears. I am just so thankful for your life and how you are a servant who loves me and my Son so much. You have given up your whole life to serve me. You have pursued me and have found my heart. You have climbed right up into my lap, and I love you so much that I come to earth to speak to you face to face. You are a treasure to me. I want you to know that you are welcome to come home. I want you to choose to stay to minister to more people. I want you to pour out your life like a drink offering. I want you to walk like my apostles who started the church.

I know that you want to die. I know that you want to come home to heaven with me. I know that you want to leave this world. But like Paul, I want you to stay and continue to minister to my people. I want you to write at least another sixty books or more. I want you to minister to the church and lead them into a relationship with me. I want you teach people how to walk like you.

Yes, heaven knows who you are. Every single person in heaven knows who you are, and they are all praying for you. I know it is painful for you to stay, but I want to use you to bring change to my church. I want you to champion and coach your readers. I want you to bring change to how people think. I have big plans for you. One day, when you are home with me and the saints in heaven, the reward will be so worth it. Part of your reward will be having people come up to you all the time in heaven and thanking you for what you did for them.

I want you to know that you are blessing me so much. I am so very thankful for your life. I am just in tears when I think of my love for you. You can see me crying. Let this image burn into your memory. Oh yes, you made me laugh, and you made me cry. I am so overwhelmed by your life. You are perfect, holy, and set apart for me. I love you so much. I love you so, so much. The word *love* is not adequate to express my feelings for you. That is why I keep on bursting into tears. I love you so much, my boy. I love you as much as I love Jesus.

You have heard before in books that I love people like I love Jesus. But here I am with my hands outstretched to you and tears running down my face. I love you, son.

You have a book coming out next month called *Gaining Freedom from Sex Addictions: Breaking Free from Pornography and Prostitutes*. That book will be out before this conversation is made into a book. I am so proud that you are going to release that book as it will help so many people. I am so happy that you could encourage people how to overcome their addictions. I am going to repay the enemy for stealing all the money that you spent on those addictions. I am going to use you to bring many people to freedom. I love this book that you will produce.

You do so much that makes me thankful. I am one of your biggest fans in heaven. It is pretty hard to compete with the love that Jesus has for you. Ha, ha.

You thought this post was going to be about you giving thanks and that I would talk about how important it is. Here we are at the end, and most of what was said was me speaking about how thankful I am for you in my life. As you can see, being thankful is a good thing. Love you heaps.

Goodbye.


Matthew:

Thanks, Dad.

# Message 7 - Carrying Burdens

God:

How are you doing today?

Matthew:

I have been struggling with sleeping too much. This could really get me down, so today, I decided to stay up all night and break the cycle. You know me; no matter what comes against me, I get through it.

God:

Yes, we are proud of you. You are an overcomer and quite resilient. I love your attitude toward life. No matter what you go though, you still seem to love me, and you don't seem to complain too much to me or others.

You are a joy to me, Matthew. I delight in you. I am really excited to talk to you. I have been calling for you to sit down and have a conversation with me in front of other people for a few days.

Sure, we have chatted back and forth as you lay in your bed, but as for my words being recorded and in print, I have been calling you to come away with me for a few days. I am glad that you are up and about, awake, and not too tired so that you can type what I have to say.

Do you know that I enjoy you? Do you know that I enjoy who you are? I look forward to the days when you are meeting more people and spreading my light to the world. I look forward to showing the world what love is through you.

I am so excited to speak to you. Once again, I have come down to speak to you face to face.

Matthew:

Misty Edwards just sang, "Oh, that you would rend the heavens and come down," and right at the same time, you came down through the portal in my kitchen.

I enjoy the look of love on your face, my Papa. I don't often call you *Papa*, but my heart is healing slowly.

I am blown away that each time I sit down to type your conversations, you are making a habit of coming down to see me. I am so shocked that you love me so. I am so overcome.

God:

I am with you in this moment. I am with you in trying times. I know you are a little worried about your test results tomorrow. I don't want you to worry. Now drink the rest of your coffee so that you can sit on your sofa and rest as you type.

That is better. Now you are relaxed. Now we can talk about carrying burdens. You carry a few of them, don't you?

Matthew:

Yes, I do carry burdens in my heart. My life is consumed with my concern for the Body of Christ. Sometimes I feel that my life has been poured out like the drink offering that Paul spoke about in his letters.

I don't know what it is. It's hard to quantify what I feel. The church and the body are dead, lukewarm, and not very well fed, and I have this massive burden for them. I care for them. My heart weeps for them. So many do not know you well. So many of them are caught up with the world and its lusts. So many people have no desire to follow Jesus and what he taught. I am saddened that even with big popular preachers in the world and thousands and thousands of books and videos, the people seem to be blind.

I am so sad. It keeps me from sleep.

For one, I feel these days that the lukewarm are not going to go to heaven unless they repent, change their ways, and live a totally different life. As Matthew 7:23 says, I feel that Jesus will say to some Christians, "Depart from me, I never knew you." If the lukewarm will be rejected and vomited out of the kingdom and the ones that run after lusts will be rejected, I am saddened for all the followers that will be rejected also.

You said once that my burden will never leave me. Is that true?


God:

Why would I lift that burden from you, my son? If the world needs to be taught and if you are one of my faithful teachers that is bringing forth my truth, why would I remove that burden from you?

What I love about you is that we have given you our heart, and you have not rejected it. Your heart beats with our love and our compassion. You have a heart for everyone. You might not agree with everyone. You may not accept what everyone says, but you do love everyone.

You have said this so many times in the prophecies that you give people, but you are a light on a hill. You are the very light of Christ on earth. You are Jesus on this earth.

Sure, you have your faults, failings, and weaknesses. You are not perfect in the world's eyes, but you are pretty good in my eyes.

I love you so much. I love you so much that you make me cry when I think about you.

You are my Enoch. I wish that I could bring you home right now. I wish that your destiny and your purpose on earth were finished and that I could take your hand and take you back to heaven with me now.

I can't help but cry for you. I love you so much. I am undone.


Matthew:

I used to see John Paul Jackson cry when I met him, and now you are crying when you speak of your love for me. Your tears mean so much to me. I imagine that it is hard for a person to read and believe this. But the readers can have faith that I tell the truth.

I think that I have made my peace with staying here. I might have more work to do on that subject, but I think I have overcome that thought. I heard you say that you want me to write another sixty books, which will take me some time.

I am so happy to meet you today. I am happy that I stayed up and sat down to speak to you. You even picked the music of Misty Edwards for me to play while I typed, which has given me some really great songs to listen to.


God:

People assume that when Jesus was on earth, his words were for the people and the leaders of that time. When he said that the blind were leading the blind, people read that and assume that he was speaking about the teachers of his day.

Some people accept that blind leaders exist today, but they aren't so quick to accept that the very leaders that they are listening to are the blind leaders he spoke about. People think that everyone is wrong except themselves and their church.

Jesus said in Revelation that the church has a so-called reputation for being alive, but that, in fact, they were dead. Under that reasoning, the churches that have the biggest reputations in the world have the most to worry about.

The reason that I will give you my heart and our burdens is because it is time for you to lead your readers to the living water in Christ and the water of the Holy Spirit. You need to lead people into a personal relationship with us. It is time for people to find us and follow us and to stop relying on other teachers for their information.

I will give each person a burden to carry and to work with. For some, it might just be a song that I want recorded. For some, it might be a blog post that I want written, and the burden will lift when that is done. I will give a larger burden to others. I will give some a mantle and a burden that will last all of their lives.

I know that what you carry is heavy for you, but it pushes you right into our bosom. You are kept close with what is on your heart and with what you carry. Be at peace. I take my leave. Go and edit this as best as you can and post it on your blog.


Matthew:

See ya.


God:

Bye for now.

# Message 8 - Feeling Down

God:

How are you, Matthew?

Matthew:

I was in bed, talking to you and about to go to sleep for the night. I felt this yearning to engage in deeper conversation with you. During this time, your Holy Spirit told me to get up and do the next chapter in this book. So here I am. I am in a good mood at the moment.

God:

First of all, I want to acknowledge your obedience. I love the fact that you are led by the Holy Spirit in many of your actions. I wish that the whole church would learn how to walk in the Holy Spirit and know how to be led by him to action each day.

I also want to thank you for keeping the title of this chapter and not for skipping a chapter as we are following the same chapters in the book, *Jesus Speaking Today*. You might not be sad at the moment, but as I start to tell you of some of the things that make me sad, you might be overcome.

Matthew:

I had a feeling that might be the case. I welcome you to my house as you sit down on the sofa opposite me. I like speaking with you face to face. Sometimes I feel like Moses and you are coming down to meet me each time that I do one of these conversations that will be written and published in a book. It's so good to see you today. I can see tears running down your face right now. What is it?


God:

Oh, it is just you saying that you feel you are like Moses. It reminds me of when the Israelites were in bondage in Egypt, and I raised them up and delivered them. They were no sooner free when they started to complain to Moses and wanted to go back to Egypt.

By and large, the church today has been shown the Promised Land. They have all the keys to access the promise, but they choose to live in bondage. I would love to visit the average believer and speak to them face to face, but they either don't believe that it is possible, or they don't maintain a culture in their lives that allows me to bring my habitation to their house.

I cry because everything has already been done for them. Everything that needed to be done has been done for them to live under an open heaven. I have not changed. Jesus made it possible. You don't need to be a prophet to speak with me face to face. I love people so much more than they know. But they seem to prefer their televisions and Facebook to spending time with me.

It breaks my heart and really makes me sad that people cannot hear me speak. They don't know my voice, and they don't know how to be led by the Holy Spirit. I need my people to hear from me. I need my people to listen to me and to do what I tell them. I need them to rely on me and follow my leading just like Jesus did when he was on earth.

I get so sad. It breaks my heart that the people who are supposed to know me don't really know me. It hurts me to see them ignore me. It hurts me to see Christians fighting and arguing and blocking each other on Facebook. I need my people to know me and be led by my Holy Spirit. I need my people to rise up and show each other love and unite and pour out my love to the world.

The world really needs my love. How are people supposed to come to know me if the Christians in the world won't be Jesus's love and Jesus's hands and feet?

Matthew:

I see your tears and feel your pain. I try my very best to show your love and teach people how to live an effective Christian life. My favorite book that I have written is called *Influencing Your World for Christ*. Yet it is one of my lowest selling books. I guess that people are simply not that interested in influencing their world for Jesus. It is sad. I feel your pain.

God:

I share your pain. I know how you feel about that book. I too would love it if lots of people bought that book and applied it, but what you say is true. Anything to do with evangelism is not popular among Christians.

Matthew, can I tell you this?

I love your heart. You have such a pure heart. Your heart is aligned to us and to our will for the earth. You might not be well known on earth, but you have made an impact in heaven. You might not feel that you are having much of an impact, but I can tell you that you are powerfully affecting a lot of lives.

You have had three people, three friends that you have met through Facebook. They read your books and have told you that you have powerfully affected their lives. Lisa, Andrea, and Mary all state that their lives are simply not the same since reading more than fifteen of your books.

So many people are just like them that you do not know. I have touched so many lives with your books. You really are making the earth a better place. You are really equipping my people to be better and more effective in their lives.

I am so proud of you and so happy with you. I wish that we could sit down every day and talk like this. I don't wish it for your sake but for mine. I would really love to hang out with you every day. You give me a reason to live. You give me a reason to hope. One day in the future, I will turn a few more people of the world onto you, and your catalogue of books will disciple many people. You will raise up an army. I will put a whole army to flight because of you. Their time won't be wasted by reading what you write as nothing that you write is a waste.

When I am feeling down in heaven, I just look at your life, and I cry and wish that I could model the world after you. Sure, some popular teachers and preachers in the world have a bigger audience than you do, but not many authors have people who buy fifteen or more of their books.

You are so obedient. You trust us for finances, so you price your books at ninety-nine cents. Instead of buying a book by popular author for $10, people buy ten of your books. That is so smart. It is such a God thing for you to do.

Yes, I want you to know that when I am feeling down, I simply watch scenes from your life. Just as Jesus has a music box that plays hologram images of your life, I too have my own room where I watch your life.

Do you know that the saints of heaven all want to meet you? Do you know that they are all lined up to meet you? Do you know that you not only interview them and make books about them and their answers, but they come back to heaven and brag about you and how they met you? When their book is released, we throw a party in heaven and play the audio book that you produced on earth. You could write another sixty books simply by interviewing saints from heaven.

You are never going to run out of books to do. Smith Wigglesworth, Kathryn Kuhlman, Charles Finney, and John G. Lake are looking forward to your next book with the great cloud of witnesses. They know that you don't know about healing, and you don't know anything about their lives, but they know you are a talented interviewer, and they have a powerful message for earth. That is going to be your next book after the book with John the Apostle.

Don't focus on open doors to preach, don't look at which book is going to be a best seller, just live each day as the Holy Spirit leads you. Focus on being obedient to us each day, and we will work out all the rest in the right time. Please don't worry about people that leave your life. We have new people to replace them. I know it hurts you, but our way is really the best.

I see that you are really nervous to interview the generals of the faith. Have faith in me that everything will be okay.

Go and proofread this as best as you can and publish it on your blog. I am happy that you are happy. You needed to know these things.


Matthew:

Bye, Papa.


God:

Bye, my son.

# Message 9 - Trust and Obey

God:

How are you doing?

Matthew:

I am pretty good tonight. I can't sleep. I have slept too much today. I am now motivated and led to have another conversation with you. I enjoyed our conversation so much yesterday. People who read it on Facebook liked it also. That is always a great sign.

God:

It is great and so positive when you receive feedback on what I say to you. I want to move you into a place where you will just hear from me and speak for me, no matter what feedback you receive. I have been moving you to a place where you don't need as much feedback on the prophecies that you give people now. You used to require a lot of feedback. Now you don't need as much feedback because your confidence that you are hearing from me has grown.

Satan is always attacking you. He likes to tell you that your prophetic gift is no good. He likes to say that your prophecies are all the same and that you have no variety in them. He hates it when you prophesy to people because he knows how powerful it is, so he wears you down by telling you that you are not as skilled at your gift as others you admire. He has you comparing yourself to others, which leads you to think that you are no good at all. He simply wants to discourage you.

I want you to know that you carry the voice of my son Jesus with all your prophecies, and they really encourage people. I want to say that I really love your gift. Like James Goll said of you, your prophecies don't just come from giftedness, but they come from a place of real humility and love. You made him cry when he heard his prophecy. You made Heidi Baker cry also. I want you to know that you don't make my generals cry without carrying my Son's words and anointing.

You deal with so many attacks. But you continue. You make me so proud of you. You are not the smartest or the most educated person. You don't know the Bible as well as some people. You struggle with mental illness. You struggle from a life full of pain and suffering. Yet you carry on and do what you are called to do.

So many times, I have seen you tired and not in the mood to prophesy, and you have started to refund their money and tell them that you are not feeling well. You have then been stopped by your compassion for them. You think how sad it would be for them to feel rejected by you, and you think how if it were you, you wouldn't want to have your money returned and not receive your prophecy, so you decide to not cancel the request and to prophesy instead.

You trust in us. When you feel that you are not adequate, you trust us. When you feel that you are not up to prophesying, you lean on the Holy Spirit. Many of those prophecies that you almost cancel turn out to be very powerful. The enemy seems to know when a powerful prophecy will be released, and he makes you tired and worn out. But most of the time, you push through, and people are really blessed. Most of them don't even know that they almost didn't get a prophecy.

You have no real idea of your future. You don't know how you will cope with traveling to other countries and adjusting and sleeping at night and ministering to people. You have no idea how your health will be. You have so many unanswered questions when it comes to your future.

You simply trust us. You simply trust us with everything that we lead you to do. When we ask you to do something, you obey without question. When we lead you, you cooperate. You simply believe that we know what is best for you. You have no idea when doors will open to preach. You have no idea when your prophecies will come true. You have no idea when you will become really popular. And you have no idea how you will handle all the attention when you do become very sought after and busy.

All you know is that we have your life planned. All you know is what to do each day. All you know is to obey the leading of the Holy Spirit each day. You have such a simple faith. You simply trust us. You have so many unanswered questions, yet still you trust us and obey us. You simply do what you feel the Holy Spirit leading you to do each day and at every hour.

Some people might think that you have it all together. Some people who have read your books look at your life and think that they would love to have a life like yours. Many of them have no idea that you have worries and concerns that weigh on you. They might think that you are some sort of super Christian, and in some ways you are, but they don't know your struggles and concerns each day.

I guess that is why it is good for me to speak to you like this. I wish that the world could know that I am not a far-off God who does not see things or care for people. I see every part of your life. I know everything that you are doing every day. I see each day when you call your special friend, Mary. I see how much pleasure you receive from having a friend who has read your books. I see each day when you struggle with your sleep. I know your every thought and your every concern. I know; I see, and I care.

I don't think people know that I care about them. I think that most people think that I am too busy in heaven to care about what is going on in their lives. I think that many people still think that I am an angry God. I am sure that many people think that they can't approach me while they are struggling with sin in their lives. Many people have no idea of who I am or what I am thinking about. They don't know me.

Oh, how I wish that other people could simply sit down and type my words and hear me speak. I wish that people could be my friend. I have feelings also. I have concerns and cares and things that discourage me. I have a world full of children that don't know me. It is not meant to be like this. People should know me. People should be able to hear from me. People should grow to become my friends as you have.

I don't want to be alone anymore. I don't want people singing praises and praying one-way prayers to me. Sure, that is nice and helpful, but there is so much more. There is so much more. I have so much to say to people. I have so much on my heart. I have so many things that I want to say to people. I have so many thoughts for their lives and directions for them.

I want to be personal with people. I want to be able to come down and sit and talk to them face to face. I want to be able to visit them and speak to them like a friend. I want to celebrate with them and cry with them. I want to comfort them and lead them. I want to see each person become everything that they are destined to become. I want to help people and be relevant to their lives.

I don't want to be some distant entity in heaven. I don't want to be a far-off God. I don't want to be just a figurehead. I don't want to be treated as a remote God. I want to have friends. I want people to really know me and speak with me. I want to be a part of their lives. I want to intimately share their lives with them.


Matthew:

This book is called *Conversations with God*, but this time you had a lot to say. I took a break to answer two chat messages on Facebook that came in. I am not sure that people really know all of this about you. I think people think that you are always joyful, happy, and contented in heaven.

I think these conversations are not only helpful for me to have with you, but they show aspects of you and your feelings that people might never have considered before.

God:

I have so much to share with you, Matthew. People need to see that this subject is trust and obey. They need to see that you trust me with your future even though you don't know how it will work out for you. You simply trust me.

People also need to see that you continue to obey me in everything. Even though you have struggles, fears, and concerns, you still obey us with your life. Each day, you sit down to do what we put on your heart to do. Each day, you go about doing what you are led to do. We love that about you. One day, when you work it out, you will write a book on how to walk in the Spirit and how to do what he says during every part of your day.

You have had struggles and sins that you have battled with for so many years, but we have loved you through all of it. You have felt dirty and unworthy to be loved, yet through all of that time, you have trusted and obeyed us in all that we asked of you. I am so thankful for you. You are so faithful to us. Many are called, but few of them can be trusted. You are trusted by us.

You can close this conversation now and try and proofread it and post it on your blog. It has become a little long. I got carried away pouring out my heart to you. You can do another conversation if you feel up to it later tonight. I want you to stay up tonight for a while. Love you, Matthew.

Matthew:

I love you, Dad

God:

Bye for now. Post this.

# Message 10 - The Journey

God:

How are you?

Matthew:

As you know, I went and tried to sleep, but I couldn't get to sleep. I was not tired enough yet to be able to sleep. Earlier tonight when we talked, I thought that we would have another conversation. And here we are now.

God:

This subject is the journey. You have been on quite the journey with your life. If people are interested in your life, they can read your memoir, *His Redeeming Love: A Memoir*. You have had a challenging life so far. I guess you have had no choice but to press on.

You have certainly battled with hardship and sin in your life. You are still receiving healing so that you can cope better. The enemy really wanted to shut you down and stop you from being an effective minister of the gospel.

I have always been overseeing what happens in your life. Through all the years of darkness and trouble, I was there, caring for you, even though you never spoke directly to me. You had a relationship with Jesus, and through Jesus, you were speaking to me. I am so happy that we can speak now. We are getting to know each other and growing closer and closer to each other.

I am so happy with your progress and with the way that you keep on learning and reading. I love how you hunger and thirst for more of me and the supernatural. Sometimes you think about when you were a new baby Christian, and you are happy with where you are now and that you are not back there. I will look after the new Christians.

Following my Son is never a boring adventure if you put your heart into it. I guess that not all teachers and pastors know how to educate and train their people. I am so glad that we have the Holy Spirit to teach, lead, and counsel people. The Holy Spirit is so kind, humble, and such a gentle teacher.

You know from experience that the Holy Spirit will allow you to be deceived for a time, but when the time is right, he will show you the truth. People don't understand it, but one can grow so much and learn many lessons from being deceived. In your life, you were once deceived for sixteen years, thinking that you were one of the two witnesses of Revelation 11. You read the Bible a lot during that season, including the books of the prophets. We allowed you to go through that. We had a reason for it. You grew to be a better person, and you ended up becoming humble and teachable after all of that.

When you have been deceived and deluded for a time, you have grace for other people that are in deception. The problem with many people who are being deceived is that they have pride issues that won't allow them to see the truth.

But we know how to teach in every situation that our people find themselves in. For sixteen years, you thought it was up to you to save and judge the world. During that time, we broadened your perspectives and allowed you to see what needs to be done in the world. Nothing in our kingdom is wasted. We use everything in a person's life.

Yes, you have had a really funny and different life. You have been led astray by familiar spirits, by false doctrine, and by delusions of grandeur, yet here you are, speaking to me. You are happy, content, hopeful, and full of faith. You are a product of your past, and you are stronger than ever. You have faith that I know what I am doing in your life.

You have no fear of being deceived as you know that even if you are, it will all work out for your good anyway (see Romans 8:28). You have complete confidence in us to lead you. You have built up your faith to such a place that we can use you to say anything that we want you to say. We can use you to interview saints that you don't know anything about, and you have the confidence that even though you don't know anything about their lives, they will speak the truth to you, and you won't be in error.

In all people's lives, we are weaving a fine tapestry and making something beautiful. We are working in their lives without them even knowing that we are working. We are even pursuing people that are not pursuing us. We are marvelous, and we have great plans for people even if they are not currently aware of them. (See Jeremiah 29:11.)

We work to see perfection formed in believers. We work to see Christ formed in people. We work to help them grow closer and closer to us. It can't happen with one prayer or one service or even one blog post or a chapter in a book, but it can and does happen. We work to answer prayers of all the faithful mothers who have prayed for their children.

A son or daughter can stray for twenty-five years and become involved in drugs, alcohol, and prostitutes and can live a totally reprobate life, yet the mother's prayers can eventually lead them back to us. Of course, not all come back to us; after all, people have free will, but you would be surprised at how many mothers' prayers we answer.

You are the result of your mother's prayers, Matthew. For many years, she has been pouring out her heart to me over your life, and now as she is old, she is starting to see the wonderful fruits of her prayers blossom. Imagine where you will be in ten or twenty years. You wrote *His Redeeming Love: A Memoir* some years ago. People will read that in ten years and see where you came from. People will be in absolute shock when they see where you came from and what you went through.

Yes, life is a journey. It does not all happen at once or in one instant, and everyone has hope to turn around and become someone that brings me praise and honor. Everyone can do things that bring me glory. No matter who they are, no matter what sins they have committed, no matter how deceived they have been, or how deceived they currently are, they can all bring me glory, and I can be proud of them.


Matthew:

I am still learning to walk totally free from sin, and this is so comforting to me to hear. I am so happy that I can bring glory to your name and be used to teach people, equip people, and build them up even while I am a work in progress.


God:

You make me very happy. You have written thirty-two books as you write this post. Last month, over two thousand people bought a book from you. You are doing a marvelous job with your life. Right now, you arranged for your books to be made available at Barnes & Noble, and soon, you will see sales through them. You are a total joy to me. Once again, you can see me crying. I receive so much joy in reflecting on your life. You have not had an easy journey in your life, but you are making it into something really worthwhile, and you are keeping some people really entertained with your books.

Can you imagine what might happen if you ever produced a best seller on the *New York Times* list? Can you imagine what would happen to all your book sales? Just think about that for a moment. How would your life change?

I love people so much. You are doing everything like we planned for it to happen. I would love for everyone to walk in our will. I would love for people to hear us speak like we speak to you. I have so many things that I would love.

People are mistaken if they think that I get everything that I want just because I am God. All of the hurt and all the abuse in the world is not my will. It is not my will for people to go to hell, but I wish that all men would come to salvation. Because I gave men free will, I have to suffer the consequences of that freedom that I granted them. People like you make me smile. My life is a whole lot more bearable when I have people obeying and trusting me with their lives.

I also enjoy it when people have faith in me no matter what is going on in their lives. I love it when people trust me no matter what hard thing they are going through. It makes my heart glad when people praise me when all hell is breaking loose around them. I enjoy the praises of people when they could instead choose to be angry and upset with me. I love the faith of people who worship and obey me despite the personal pain that they are in. I enjoy people like you, my son.

Thank you for listening again today, Matthew.


Matthew:

It was an honor. Have a wonderful day in heaven.

God:

Bless you, son.

## Message 11 - Life's Hurdles

God:

How are you?

Matthew:

I slept for most of yesterday, so I couldn't sleep tonight. I have been up for most of the night. I just felt led to speak to you. Welcome to my house.

God:

I really enjoy coming to speak to you. You are a joy to me. What you consider as faults and sins in your life that you allowed to keep you from intimacy with us were only in your life for a season. Now you are doing really well. You have a testimony that can encourage and inspire so many people.

People love you as a writer as you share your life with all your struggles and hurdles. People only have to read the beginnings of each post to see that you have sleep issues in your life.

Your life is not normal, and you would struggle to hold down a normal job because of your sleep issues. People are encouraged when they see that you have a life that has its own struggles as they see that your life is not perfect, and therefore, they too can reach the sort of relationship that we have also. Leaders shouldn't give the impression that their life is out of reach and unattainable.

Matthew:

Many people who read my books report to me in emails and through reviews that they admire my honesty and transparency. I think that the best way to give people an atmosphere where they can learn is to be vulnerable. I certainly enjoy being taught by people who are up front about the hurdles and struggles that they go through in life.

Life seems to have one challenge after another to deal with. We are certainly not in a straight race in life. Life has many hurdles that we have to get over. It is not always easy.

I am going away for five days next week on a ministry trip to someone's home, and I am worried that I will sleep too much, and they will think that I am lazy. I know these thoughts are simply coming from the enemy that is trying to get me into fear.


God:

It will be a nice visit for you next week. You will do well, and they won't judge you. We will work with you so that you will enjoy yourself. The enemy often has you worry, and we can understand that because even tonight, you are up, and your sleep patterns are affected. You will be okay, though. We will work with you.

We are going to make sure that you are anointed and that you are led by our Spirit so that you can really touch Honni and show her that you really are a special person. We are going to work with you and be with you. You can be sure that we will work with you so that you impress her.

You hold yourself in little regard. You really do not know how awesome you are. Your friend, Lisa, tells you that you have really no idea about how impressive that you are. She has read fifteen of your books, and she is impressed with you, but when she talks to you, she realizes that you do not have a big ego because she sees that you don't really have any concept of how awesome you are.

Matthew:

Thank you, my Lord. Thank you for speaking to me and reminding me of that part about myself. I have to agree that I don't really understand what is so special about me.

I know that many people don't speak to you face to face like I do. I know many people don't talk to saints like I do and have the opportunity to interview them. I know that not many people are as close to Jesus as I am. But I know that all of this is possible for people if they desire it. I have not done anything that others can't do.

I guess people don't want to suffer the life that I have suffered. I guess people don't want to leave the world and its lusts and become separated unto you. I guess people don't want to put the time into getting to know you and Jesus like I do. I guess it is too hard for people, so they put up with their situation.

God:

You are unique. You are special and rare in the kingdom. Let me tell you that you mean a lot to me. You even meant a lot to me before you overcame your sins. You have a pure heart, a heart like David. Like David, your writings are encouraging others to draw closer to me. I enjoy you. One of my favorite things is to come down here and speak to you.

You are like Moses to me. One day, you will see how many people you are affecting, and you will see that I spoke the truth to you here and now. I come down to meet with you face to face like I did with Moses because you are a special friend to me. I enjoy speaking to you and sharing my life with you.

I wish that people would prepare their own hearts to welcome me. I wish that I could come and visit with all of my people. I wish that people really wanted me to come and see them. I wish that all people could be as friendly to me as you are, my friend. It is my hope through these books that people might come to see my heart and my desire to fellowship with them.

Coping with life and its many hurdles is a whole lot easier when you know me and when you have a living relationship with me. I can make any person's life easier when they know me, and I give them my favor. I want to bless people, but so many of them are my enemies, loving the world and its ways more than they love me (James 4:4).

I have so much that I could do for people. I have so much to share with them. I have so much love that I want to pour into them. My heart aches for them. If people only knew how much I wanted to bless them and go before them in life and open doors for them: doors of prosperity, doors of blessing, and doors of favor (Jeremiah 29:11). I have so much to give to them if they would only let go of the world and its lusts. If they would only let go of their selfishness and die to self. If only my people would do things the way that I have planned for them (1 John 2:15-17).

I get sad sometimes as I speak to you, Matthew. You are so kind and so open with me. You allow me to speak my heart and don't shut me down. You don't have any agenda and any desire to ask me for things and seek your own will. It's easy to speak to you, and you really listen to me. You don't switch off your mind to think of other things, and you don't ask me to speak about other things. I come to your place, and you simply allow me to speak and unburden myself. What is more, your readers will read what I have to say and will also hear my heart. That makes me happy.

I wish the world would discover you as an author and publish your books far and wide so that many more people would be blessed by what you write. People assume that I control everything, but mankind still has a lot of control in the world. We could show your books to someone with a major publishing firm, yet it would still be up to that person to see the value of your books and reach out to you.

You have no idea how happy it makes me to come down here and meet with you face to face and to share my heart with you. You make me so happy. You bring me so much joy. My life in heaven is so much richer, knowing that I have you on earth. You are my precious son. I really wish that you could capture how much I love you.

On an earlier visit, I actually cried when I told you that I loved you, and that showed you my love, but that still does not even cover it. You are so precious to me.

It is time to finish this, or it will be too long. Thank you for listening to me.


Matthew:

It is my pleasure, God.


God:

See you later. Try and proofread this and post it.

# Message 12 - Trouble

God:

How are you doing today?

Matthew:

Once again, it is in the middle of the night right now. I am going to try and stay up today so that my sleep can return to normal. It's so funny for people to read. They must wonder if I ever sleep correctly.

God:

Perhaps your sleeping cycle is an image of the normal Christian life. Perhaps people have their understanding of the Christian life all backwards. When they should be talking to us, perhaps they are relying on men and other solutions. I guess the people of God would enjoy having a relationship like you have. They would like your relationship to be normal to them.

I enjoy coming down to see you, Matthew. It is so good to come and sit on your sofa and speak to you. I like how I can just be myself around you, and I don't have to be careful how I speak to you and speak through your doctrine or your beliefs to better communicate with you. I love how I can just share my heart with you and eventually your readers.

Matthew:

I would like to think that I make most people feel like that. I hope that I make most people feel comfortable to share what is on their mind. I am pretty open and loving, and I hope that I demonstrate grace wherever I go.

But it is so good to hear that you feel comfortable enough to speak your mind freely with me. I would not want you to think that you have to speak like an Old Testament God. I enjoy you speaking to me in easy-to-understand, down-to-earth language. I guess some people might not think that you can speak like this.


God:

I am the same as any human. If you were talking about golf, you would have a certain language that you would use to talk to another golfer. As a Christian, you talk to other Christians on different levels, depending on their walk. If you were a scientist and if you were talking to a scientist, you would talk in a specific way.

You are a simple person. You like to speak simply, so I speak in your language and your words so that you can understand. I can talk to a golfer; I can talk to a theologian, and I can speak to a scientist, and no matter where a person is coming from, I can speak to them right where they are at. I know all things.


Matthew:

That is amazing. You know all things. I am not sure I would want to know all things. It seems like too much responsibility would be involved in knowing everything. I am happy just to know what I know and to slowly increase in knowledge and understanding as time goes on.

I have had people comment to me that they enjoy the simplicity of your messages. I guess in their simplicity, they can be quite profound.

God:

There is great wisdom in keeping things simple. Jesus told simple parables, yet they are quite profound once you look into them. The trick is having the courage to be simple in the way that you communicate. Some people are so educated that they cannot help themselves from speaking in a complex way. That is fine if your readers are also educated people, but it can be an issue for people like you to try and read.

I enjoy you because you are simple with no pretenses. You have an amazing relationship with Jesus, one that is very rare, but you don't boast in it or try and make other people feel bad that they don't have the same relationship that you have.

It is sad to say that some people are proud and cannot help communicating with that pride. It has been many years and a lot of trials and tests, but we have dealt with most of your pride. You have become a sweet ambassador of Jesus Christ to this world.

I want you to know that I enjoy you. This world has a lot of troubles, and many people are in dire straits. So much trouble is going around. It is really heartbreaking to be God and to have to see and experience all the heartache in the world. It really causes me a lot of pain. I suffer watching it all with no way to help people.

Can you imagine a father knowing that his young daughter has been abducted and is being used as a child prostitute? That would break the father's heart. But imagine if the father had to watch his daughter abused and raped by men and could not do anything about it. That father would suffer so much anguish.

Well, Matthew, I am that father. I watch millions and millions of people being abused all day, every day. So many times, the people who are being abused cannot be set free. Sometimes people are suffering, and a Christian could reach out to them and help them, but the Christian doesn't even acknowledge them or their suffering. What breaks my heart is that the world could have a whole lot less suffering in it if the church and Christians weren't so selfish with their money and how they choose to spend it, yet they don't ever seem to get the message.

People can be homeless and suffering right in front of their eyes, and many of my people will not even look at them or acknowledge them in their suffering, let alone give them something to eat or take them in.

I am overcome by the trouble and the suffering in the world. When people suffer, I suffer. I guess the people of God don't really know that I suffer or else they might do something about it. I get so sad. According to many people, it is almost blasphemy for me to say that I suffer and that I am sad. The concept people have of God does not include God weeping and getting down. They have this idea that heaven is full of praise and worship and that I am joyful all the time.

That is why it is so refreshing for me to be able to come to earth and speak to you and not hold anything back. I don't have to be anything special or twist your arm to listen to me. I don't have to hide my feelings. We simply try to stay on one topic for each chat so that the book has some order, yet you allow me to speak.

Matthew:

It breaks my heart to see you cry, Father. It breaks my heart. I have to put this hurt in a separate compartment so that I can handle it. There is so much hurt and trouble in this world because of religion and what the teachers have taught the people.

You are right. Most people would not have any concept that you are in pain and that you see the troubles in the world. In the world, we have two types of prophets speaking about the recent hurricanes in the U.S. Some prophets claim that it is your judgement, and others say that you would never do that.

68

I am not going to ask you which is which, but I am saddened that not even your prophets can agree on your behalf. So many people have suffered because of the destruction, and surely, that must hurt you.


God:

Yes, that is another whole topic when my prophets are saying two different things. The actual people who are meant to have my ear on things cannot agree. That saddens me.

It also upsets me that the teachers and pastors in the world teach garbage that I don't have feelings like a normal father does. People not only suffer, but they also think that I don't really even care about their suffering.

Can you imagine how the victims of the hurricanes feel, thinking that I sent them? It must break their heart to think that I did that. I am so happy that I have you to talk to, a friend that helps me process through my feelings. I am so happy to have you as my friend. I am excited that you make these conversations into books and actually sit down and type them. Not only can you hear me speak, but other people can tune in and listen to what we have to say to each other.

I am not sure that you really understand how much I enjoy coming down to see you. I am growing deeper and deeper in love with you. You are really touching my heart. You will always be my friend. I will always be your friend. I enjoy speaking to you so much.

Your new book, _How to Hear God's Voice: Keys to Two-Way Conversational Prayer_, is coming out soon, and I know that will help so many people start to have conversations with me. I am so happy about that. The book will produce a lot of good fruit. I am so very happy with you and the way you obey me and produce the books that I want.

Matthew:

Yes, that book has been a major work and took a lot of effort to complete. Once again, a lot of warfare surrounded it. Substantial warfare seems to surround every book of mine. The enemy doesn't seem to like the books that I write.


God:

That is because heaven is ordering them to be written. You have written enough for this post now. Thank you for listening to me. I really do love you. My love for you is growing more and more each time I visit you, which is something the blind guides won't understand, either!

Bless you, Matthew.


Matthew:

Bye, Dad.

# Message 13 - Patience

God:

How are you, Matthew?


Matthew:

I am up in the middle of the night again. I have an odd sleeping schedule. It is backwards for most people; I am asleep when they are awake and vice versa. I am almost on American time. I don't worry about it too much anymore. If I worried about it, it would get to me and get me down.


God:

I asked you to look up a scripture in James 1:2-4 and post it here. Please put it here below.

"My brethren, count it all joy when you fall into various trials, knowing that the testing of your faith produces patience. But let patience have its perfect work, that you may be perfect and complete, lacking nothing."


Matthew:

I was just speaking to my mother about this verse the other day. I was telling her that I have been patient for a long time, so it must be positively impacting me. I couldn't remember what the verse said, but I knew that it was something positive.

God:

I have been molding you through patience, Matthew. You have been waiting for some things to happen for as long as forty years. You have not opened doors on your own, yet you have cried many tears as you have wished you could be used.

You have wanted to preach for forty years. You have waited patiently for me to use you. Sometimes you become upset and wring your hands in frustration, but I am using the situation to complete you and make you perfect in my love. Don't you see that now?

Matthew:

I forgot that the verse said that patience perfects a person. I can see your wisdom now. I am also grateful that you are allowing my books to reach so many people. In one way, seeing my book reach two thousand people in a month is just the same as preaching. I am having an impact on people.

God:

One day, I am going to use you to go from church to church and teach their people how to have dynamic relationships with me and Jesus and teach them how to move in the prophetic.

I have a lot for you to do. You just need to wait for me. I have my timing. I have the time where I want you to be released to the churches. I need to do work in the churches first, and I need to do work in you first.

I need you to trust me. It is not that you do not have a great message, but most churches are not ready for what you will bring to them. Sadly, many pastors don't want their congregations to be able to speak to me and be independent of them. That fact surprises you, but it is true of many pastors who are threatened by prophetic congregations that hear from me.

I am going to do a work and go before you and shift the hearts of individual pastors. I will have them start to look for people that can train their congregations. I am going to stir the hearts of the congregations to find you and your books, and they will ask their pastor to have you speak.

You don't have to really understand how it will work. One day, you will be at home writing books, and in the very next season, you will seem to be traveling all around to teach people how to hear from God and how to move in the prophetic.

You have been faithful at simply doing what I ask of you. You have endured the trials in your life, and you have been patient. Even the way that you handle your problems with your sleep schedule is commendable. You don't really complain, but you just get on with your life and cope with it.

I really love you and everything about you. You have become a great man of God. One thing I will say of you is that you are very patient. You have not only waited to preach, but you have been waiting for your future wife. You have waited a long time for her. I admire you. I really love you. You can't have the wrong wife going forward. You need to have the right support in your life and ministry and not just a woman to keep you sexually happy and comforted emotionally.

How would a wife cope with you giving your books away at ninety-nine cents? Would she agree with you while you date and when you marry but later on, put pressure on you to increase the prices? How would a wife cope with your disability pension and with you working full time for me? Would your future wife pressure you to find a job that brings in more income? Would she know that your whole life is devoted to me and ministry? As you can see, it will take a very special woman to be with you and to work with you. What if we want her to also minister with you? That means that she would need to be anointed as well. Many things come into play when finding a wife for you. It's not as simple as finding any single woman.

We are moving in your life and doing things. You might not see the movement. You might not see us moving in your life, but even as you move away from addictions, we are moving in you and for you. You are a total blessing to us. We are so happy with you. I want you to know that you please me so much, and you encourage me that other people can become as close to me as you are.

I guess that it is sometimes hard to get your focus off ministry. If I told you to stop using Facebook for three months and to quit working on books for three months, you would be seriously impacted. I am not going to ask for that, but you were panicking as I had you type those words. I just use that to show that you are already in ministry and that I am already using you to impact people. When you are forced to look at things like that, you can more readily see how I am using you, and you will have a better perspective.

People need to be patient and find out why they are here and why they are living. So many people don't know why they are here. I had you address this in your book, *Finding Your Purpose in Christ*. I hope that people read that book and use the advice in it to pursue the reason why they are here and start to apply these things in their lives. Life can be much more wholesome and enjoyable if you know why you were created.


Matthew:

Yes, I don't know how people manage without knowing why they are here. It is so important. I don't know how I would cope if

I didn't know why I was here and know that I am called to be a prophet and a writer.

You scared me when you mentioned not posting on Facebook or writing for three months. I am glad that you were using it just to make your point. I can see your point now, and I acknowledge it. You are right about my wife as well. It is not a matter of just meeting any single woman. There is so much to consider.

I really enjoy speaking with you. I enjoy how you are involved in every aspect of my life. You speak into every part of my life, and nothing that concerns me is too mundane for you. You have an idea and a way for me to do everything that I do. You are going to be with me as I go away on this ministry trip for five days. You are going to come and bring me comfort so that I can bless the people that have invited me. You have already spoken into that, and I am not as worried about it because you have spoken your peace into it.

Thank you for coming down and speaking to me today. Thank you for being with me through every part of my life. I want to bless you and praise your mighty name. I want the world to know that you are alive and powerful and a great help to all who seek you. Goodbye for today.


God:

Goodbye, Matthew.

# Message 14 - Life Dreams

God:

How are you feeling, Matthew?

Matthew:

I have had a good day. I have been listening to a new audio book, and I am learning about Facebook, Google, Amazon, and Apple. I am amazed at the success of these companies. I am sure that they are dreams come true for some people. I have just downloaded a new worship album by Steffany Gretzinger, and I am listening to it. It seems really nice. She seems to have a great heart.

God:

If you were musical, Matthew, the world would really hear some great worship from you. You would write some great songs. The world really sees how big your heart is in these conversations. You make me so happy.

You have been sad for a time this month as your book sales have been down. We had to get you focused on touching just one life and not touching the masses. We needed you to focus on us and our relationship and not on numbers.

You released a great book this week, *How to Hear God's Voice: Keys to Two-Way Conversational Prayer*. I am so proud of you laboring over that book and making sure that it was published and made available to people. That book is going to affect a lot of people so that they become closer and closer to me.

Can you imagine living a Christian life without being able to hear Jesus or me? Can you imagine the silence? How would you cope if all you had were people's books, the Bible, and one-way prayers? How would you get by?

Matthew:

I would not do well. I don't know if I could cope. I don't know how people cope without hearing from you and Jesus. I don't know how people live lives that are not directed by the Holy Spirit. I am not sure I would know how to go through a day without being led by the Holy Spirit. I don't know how people go through life without a true relationship with you guys and a two-way communication channel.

God:

The subject of this chapter is life dreams. I have a dream. I wish that I could speak to the world. Sometimes I release a book to the world, and I have some great things to say through an author, but then most of the time, I only speak to a Christian audience. The book, _The Purpose Driven Life_, really struck a chord with many people, and Rick Warren touched millions of people's lives for me.

But you live in the world with billions of people. I would love to speak to everyone and draw them to myself. Sometimes I see you wishing that your books were more popular, and this series of books would be a great message for people if they could find them. I know that you would love to see this series of books reach millions, but to be honest with you, I wish I could take this series of books to the billions.

My heart really aches for mankind. I wish that all men and women could hear me. I wish that all the people of the world could hear me speak. It is my dream. I dream of a world where everyone could hear me speak.

I am not sure that people can really grasp how much I want to be heard. I don't think that people have any idea how much I want to be friends with the people of the world.

Some people see you as a prophet and say to themselves that since you are a prophet, you are called to a closer relationship with me. They don't realize that they too can have a lasting, deep, and intimate relationship with me. You are no one special. You don't have something that other people cannot have. Oh yes, you have made sacrifices to become as close as you are to me. You have put work and effort into your relationship, and together we have shared many things that caused our relationship to become strong. But you have not done anything that they could not also do.

Perhaps you are a forerunner in intimacy with me. Perhaps I should hold you up as a model and show you off and draw others to myself through you and your example. But you don't even consider yourself better than anyone or able to do anything that others can't do. You agree with me that friendship with the God of heaven and earth is not only possible but the right choice for people to make.


Matthew:

Perhaps people are scared of you. Maybe they don't want to go to the effort. Perhaps they are worried that they will have to give up their lives and do things that they don't want to do.

All I know is that it doesn't hurt to start the conversation. It doesn't hurt to take out a journal and start to speak to you and hear what you have to say to them. It might be hard going for them at first to hear from you and to realize that you are a God with emotions and feelings and that you are real.

I hope that people who read the *Conversations with God* series of books become so encouraged that they learn to speak to you; they learn to hear from you and start to also journal with you.

In this way as people come to speak to you, I know that we are getting closer to your life's dreams. I know that you want to speak to the whole world, but perhaps more of us can share your words with other people, and our lives can be used to influence the world for Christ. They can learn how to influence their world by reading my book, *Influencing Your World for Christ*.


God:

I enjoy coming down and speaking with you. I consider you special and unique in my kingdom, but what you have achieved is possible for anyone. In that way, even though you are really special to me, the place that you are can also be reached by any determined person.

I would never want people to assume that you are some kind of elite Christian at a level that they can't possibly reach. I would like all my followers to know that they can all speak to me, meet me face to face, come to heaven, meet Jesus, be led by the Holy Spirit, move in the gifts of the Spirit, and meet and converse with angels and saints and more. You walk in so much that is also possible for other people. You speak of some of these things and pray a prayer for people in your book, *Walking under an Open Heaven.*

I really enjoy speaking to you. I know that you are not going to discard my words or treat them with contempt. You need to stay humble and close to me. You need me to visit with you and commune with you. I enjoy speaking to my friends. You have been a good friend to me. I love how you do what my Holy Spirit tells you to do. From the downloading of this album to sitting down and typing this message, I trust you to do what we tell you to do.

I will see that you achieve your life dreams as you do what I say to do from week to week. Just keep on following us, and we will see to it that you walk into your destiny. That goes for everyone that is reading also. Follow us and our leading, and you will fulfil your destiny and purpose with our help.

Matthew:

Thank you, Father. I will bid you goodnight.

God:

Goodnight, Matthew.

# I'd love to hear from you

One of the ways that you can bless me as a writer is by writing an honest and candid review of my book on Amazon. I always read the reviews of my books, and I would love to hear what you have to say about this one.

Before I buy a book, I read the reviews first. You can make an informed decision about a book when you have read enough honest reviews from readers. One way to help me sell this book and to give me positive feedback is by writing a review for me. It doesn't cost you a thing but helps me and the future readers of this book enormously.

To read my blog, request a life-coaching session, request your own personal prophecy, request a visit to heaven, or to receive a personal message from your angel, you can also visit my website at http://personal-prophecy-today.com All of the funds raised through my ministry website will go toward the books that I write and self-publish.

You can also request a trip to heaven with Robin Gann. You can find her contact information on my website.

To write to me about this book or to share any other thoughts, please feel free to contact me at my personal email address at survivors.sanctuary@gmail.com

You can also friend request me on Facebook at Matthew Robert Payne. Please send me a message if we have no friends in common as a lot of scammers now send me friend requests.

You can also do me a huge favor and share this book on Facebook as a recommended book to read. This will help me and other readers.

# How to Sponsor a Book Project

If you have been blessed by this book, perhaps you might consider sponsoring a book for me. It normally costs me between $1,500 and $2,000 or more to produce each book that I write, depending on the length of the book.

If you seek the Holy Spirit about financing a book for me, I know that the Lord would be eternally grateful to you. Consider how much this book has blessed you and then think of hundreds or even thousands of people who would be blessed by a book of mine. As you are probably aware, the vast majority of my books are ninety-nine cents on Kindle, which proves to you that book writing is indeed a ministry for me and not a money-making venture. I would be very happy if you supported me in this.

If you have any questions for me or if you want to know what projects I am currently working on that your money might finance, you can write to me at survivors.sanctuary@gmail.com and ask me for more information. I would be pleased to give you more details about my projects.

You can sow any amount to my ministry by simply sending me money via the PayPal link at this address: http://personal-prophecy-today.com/support-my-ministry/

You can be sure that your support, no matter the amount, will be used for the publishing of helpful Christian books for people to read.

# Other Books by Matthew Robert Payne

The Prophetic Supernatural Experience

Prophetic Evangelism Made Simple

Your Identity in Christ

His Redeeming Love: A Memoir

Writing and Self-Publishing Christian Nonfiction

Coping with your Pain and Suffering

Living for Eternity

Jesus Speaking Today

Great Cloud of Witnesses Speak

My Radical Encounters with Angels

Finding Intimacy with Jesus Made Simple

My Radical Encounters with Angels- Book Two

A Beginner's Guide to the Prophetic

Michael Jackson Speaks from Heaven

7 Keys to Intimacy with Jesus

Conversations with God: Book 1

Optimistic Visions of Revelation

Conversations with God: Book 2

Finding Your Purpose in Christ

Influencing your World for Christ: Practical Everyday Evangelism

Deep Calls unto Deep: Answering Questions on the Prophetic

My Visits to the Galactic Council of Heaven

The Parables of Jesus Made Simple: Updated and Expanded Edition

Great Cloud of Witnesses Speak: Old and New

Walking under an Open Heaven

A Message from My Angel: Book 1

Interviews with the Two Witnesses: Enoch and Elijah Speak

Gaining Freedom from Sex Addictions: Breaking Free of Pornography and Prostitutes

Mary Magdalene Speaks from Heaven: A Divine Revelation

Princess Diana Speaks from Heaven: A Divine Revelation

How to Hear God's Voice: Keys to Conversational Two-Way Prayer

You can find my published books on my Amazon author page here: http://tinyurl.com/jq3h893

**Upcoming Books**

Great Cloud of Witnesses Speak: God's Generals

# About Matthew Robert Payne

Matthew was raised in a Baptist church and was led to the Lord at the tender age of eight. He has experienced some pain and darkness in his life, which has given him a deep compassion and love for all people.

Today, he's an administrator in a Facebook group called "Prophetic Training Platform," and he invites you to join him there. Matthew has a commission from the Lord to train up prophets and to mentor others in the Christian faith. He does this through his Facebook posts and by writing relevant books on the Christian faith.

God has commissioned him to write at least fifty books in his life, and he spends his days writing and earning the money to self-publish. You can support him by donating money at http://personal-prophecy-today.com or by requesting any of his other services available through his ministry website.

It is Matthew's prayer that this book has blessed you, and he hopes it will lead you into a deeper and more intimate relationship with God.

CPSIA information can be obtained
at www.ICGtesting.com
Printed in the USA
LVHW110101181218
600851LV00001B/3/P